# RAILWAYS NORTH OF NOTTINGHAM IN THE LATTER DAYS OF STEAM

# Part One: *NOTTINGHAM to BASFORD*

## *Malcolm Castledine*

*BOOK LAW PUBLICATIONS*

ii

*DEDICATED TO MY MOTHER AND FATHER*
*WITHOUT WHOSE ENCOURAGEMENT AND BLESSING*
*THESE PICTURES MIGHT NOT HAVE BEEN.*

*First published in the United Kingdom by Book Law Publications 2004*
*382 Carlton Hill, Nottingham, NG4 1JA*
*Printed and bound by*
*The Amadeus Press,*
*Cleckheaton, West Yorkshire.*

# INTRODUCTION

Growing up within sight and sound of a railway installation be it a shed, junction, yard or station was something that millions of little boys had done for more than one hundred and seventy years. I grew up within sight and sound of Bagthorpe Junction in Basford, Nottingham in the post-war years when British Railways was younger than myself, and the steam locomotive was a part of everyday life.

My particular bit of BR was the former Great Central main line on the north side of the city and some of my earliest memories are of my mother taking me in my pushchair to Perry Road bridge where I could watch trains and repay mother with a beaming smile. I actually learnt to read numbers and names from the local 'namers' such as A3's 60104 SOLARIO (hard one that), 60109 HERMIT, 60111 ENTERPRISE, etc. As soon as I was allowed to go out on my own I found a favourite section of fencing where I could sit for hours trainspotting. Even when the family used to go on holiday my father and myself used to sneak off to watch the trains which were usually quite foreign to my contemporary parochial tastes but nevertheless very interesting and exciting to see.

When I was attending junior school I used to make a point of sighting the Up *MASTER CUTLER* every morning before setting foot within the school precincts. Usually, I seem to remember, it was nearly always headed by 60052 PRINCE PALATINE. It was this interest in railways generally which helped along my education and the thirst for knowledge with its mixture of curiosity. Knowing how a steam locomotive worked was one of my earliest ambitions and by the time I was ten years old I did know all there was to know, and the technical terms that went with the knowledge.

At sometime during my seventeenth year I decided that taking engine numbers was no good, or at least it did not fulfil my particular interest in railways at that time, so another decision was made and I took up railway photography.

As film and cameras were expensive then - film being 3/3d (16p) a roll - it was though prudent to learn the art and skills of photography so that I could process and print my own exposures. For reasons of cost I used monochrome in those early days and the film was processed, catalogued and stored for printing later (some 30 to 40 years later!), again for reasons of cost. Dad was a police sergeant and when the local police photographer saw my early efforts, he obviously thought that there was some potential and 'took me under his wing' teaching much which I would probably never have known otherwise. He also helped obtain equipment for my own darkroom.

Moving on to secondary education, I was fortunate in having to go to Ellis school Basford which involved me having to cross the ex Midland Leen valley line at Basford Vernon and Lincoln Street crossing. Of course I used to linger watching trains both going to school and returning home. Another bonus with this school was its high elevation on Bar Lane and I could see right across to the GC at Bagthorpe Junction.

The senior geography master at Ellis secondary was John Clarke and he too was a railway enthusiast and photographer who introduced me to the local (East Midlands) branch of the Railway Correspondence & Travel Society. I soon became a member, broadening my horizons, taking part in Sunday shed bashing trips, meetings, railtours, etc. I still keep in touch with John Clarke and we still spend time at the lineside.

Because most of the RCTS branch members were interested in number taking only, I was always last back on the bus which generated abusive and good humoured banter at every location. On one particular trip, in the early days, the Hon. Sec., a Midland man through and through, saw me with my tripod set-up deep inside Holbeck shed attempting to take a photograph of one of the last Fowler 2-6-4T's. I was greeted with a comment such as "You'll be b —— lucky". He was presented with a photograph of said engine at the next meeting. After that, they always waited (on his instructions) for me to finish photographing. I'd made my mark.

I decided to capture on film as much of the local railway scene as was possible, in particular the former Great Central line. At first I used vantage points accessible to the public such as stations, bridges, etc., and in doing so was lucky to meet many of the local railway staff. Then, in early 1964 came a turning point when I obtained a lineside photographic permit from the then local Area Manager Mr R.D.Gardner.

**Malcolm Castledine**
*Nottingham, 2004*

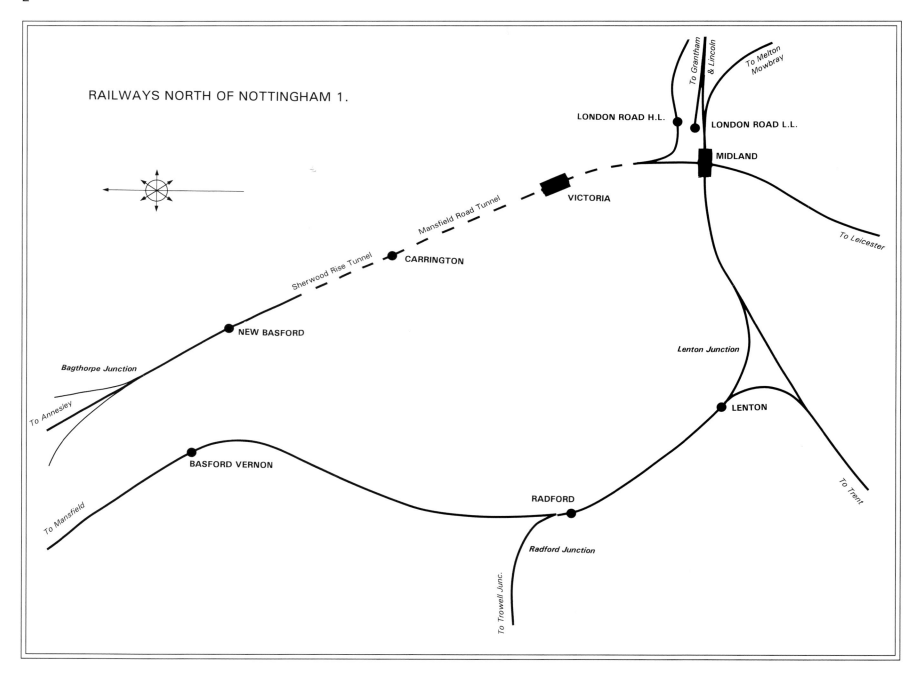

RAILWAYS NORTH OF NOTTINGHAM 1.

Nottingham (Victoria), Saturday 6th April 1963. Doncaster built Ivatt Class 4 No.43061 departs bay platform 3 with a midday service to Derby (Friargate). The 'mogul' had arrived at Colwick during the previous December with seven others of its ilk from Boston, and was to join other Ivatt 2-6-0's already on the books of 'last chance Colwick'. Whereas some of 'mogul's' managed to get away from Colwick to other sheds, 43061 did not and was condemned in January 1964. Thompson B1 No.61160, in the middle road, was the Victoria station pilot for this day and was hardly being taxed, although if the need arose it could be called upon to take over from an ailing engine on a main line express. The B1, another Colwick engine and on its third stint at the shed, was condemned on Sunday 22nd September - basically after the Summer timetable had finished.

On the same Saturday as the previous photograph, but at the south end of the station, BR Standard Cl.4 No.76052, of Woodford Halse shed, was at the head of an empty stock train on the middle siding awaiting a signal for departure to Arkwright Street carriage sidings.

Another BR Standard, but a Class 5 this time, No.73157 straddles the south end turntable on Saturday 28th December 1963 whilst its crew get stuck in to turning 130 tons of hot metal. This engine was a very recent addition to the Woodford allocation at the time and was turning here with a view to returning home without the need to replenish any coal in its tender.

Looking more the part for the period, 'Jubilee' No.45643 RODNEY of Farnley Junction shed, heads the Poole-Bradford express northwards out of Victoria on Saturday 4th July 1964. This train had arrived in Nottingham from the south headed by 'Hall' 6906 CHICHELEY HALL. Victoria station was the official changing point from Western Region to London Midland motive power. However, that was not always the case as circumstances could, and often did, change the rules. On 15th August 1964 6858 WOOLSTON GRANGE arrived at 2.35 p.m. on 1N72 Poole-Bradford. No replacement engine was available, so an Annesley crew (who would it seems drive anything) took it on to Sheffield where it displaced a platform coping stone. Here no engine was available either and the North Eastern Region driver at Sheffield refused to take it any further, so a Locomotive Inspector took the 'Grange' and its train on to Huddersfield (damaging the wooden platform at Denby Dale on the way), where it was dumped on Hillhouse shed.

(opposite) It was not the intention of this tome to illustrate 'steam specials' etc., of the period, however, there were a couple which really did require a photographic record and comment. This is one of them. The date is Saturday 9th May 1964. The venue Nottingham (Victoria) and the special - THE EAST MIDLANDER which was organised by the East Midlands branch of the Railway Correspondence & Travel Society. The locomotive is Stanier Pacific 46251 CITY OF NOTTINGHAM nicely cleaned up to show off its Crimson Lake livery. The East Midlands branch of the RCTS had a somewhat charismatic committee and one of their many organised 'events' was the annual rail tour from Nottingham to one or more of the BR locomotive works. Each year a different locomotive or locomotives would be specifically chosen as the motive power. In 1964 the appropriately named 'Duchess' headed the special from Nottingham the destination being Eastleigh works and Swindon works. At Didcot a Southern Region 'West Country' No.34038 LYNTON took over for the run to Eastleigh and then Swindon, where the 'Duchess' again took charge for the home run back to Nottingham. No.46251 was withdrawn from service, along with fifteen of the surviving Stanier Pacifics, on 12th September 1964 leaving just 46256 as the last LMS Pacific in service. However, 46256 only had three more weeks in service before it too was withdrawn and was then cut up for scrap. CITY OF NOTTINGHAM fared no better as it too was scrapped shortly after withdrawal.

A parting shot of 92120 and its rake of Southern Region green coaches as it leaves Victoria, ready to enter Mansfield Road tunnel and tackle the climb up to Bagthorpe Junction.

*(opposite)* **BR Standard 9F's from Annesley shed were no strangers on passenger trains along the Great Central route but a Crewe North 9F was very rare - so rare in fact that it was virtually impossible as Crewe North shed never had a BR Standard 9F on their books. But, that does not explain the 5A shedplate on the smokebox door of 92120 on 4th July 1964 - why was it there and which shed fixed it in place? This particular 9F was officially allocated to the Midland shed at Leicester and from that shed it could easily have got onto this working which was the 10.45 a.m. Saturdays only Poole-Sheffield. The arrival has brought with it a lot of activity on the platform both from passengers and staff. There appears to be a crew change and are those Darnall men ready to take the train forward to Sheffield (Victoria).**

With the closure of Leicester G.C. shed in July 1964, engine changing then took place at Nottingham Victoria instead of Leicester Central so western Region 'Halls' in particular, and the odd 'Grange' were seen at Victoria especially on summer Saturdays on inter-regional holiday trains and the 22nd August 1964 was perhaps typical as 'Hall' 6906 was again "about the place". Sometimes these interlopers would require a top-up of coal and would visit Annesley for such. At other times they might go up to Bagthorpe Junction to turn on the triangle if the Victoria turntable was not used. Today it looks as though 6906 did not need to leave the station as its fireman sorts out the coal in the tender whilst waiting for the return working. Black 5 No.45346 is a recent addition to Annesley's growing fleet of Stanier products having come over the wall from the other side; up until the previous July it had been a resident of the former Midland shed in Nottingham. In June 1965, just in time perhaps, the Black 5 escaped back to the LMS and went to Lostock Hall. Here the engine is about to depart platform 10 with a train for London at 5.15 p.m.

(*opposite*) Colwick B1 No.61390 takes water from the crane at the end of platform 7 on 4th July 1964. The rear aspect of the buildings on the Lower Parliament Street bridge nicely frame this engine as it replenishes its tender. The B1 is obviously local as the 'platform enders' are taking not the slightest bit of notice of it and are waiting for some rarer fare, perhaps a 'Hall' or 'Grange' from the Western. Having arrived at Colwick shed for its second stint in June 1960, after a couple of years there in the early 1950s, this engine was destined to be one of the hundreds which ended their days at Colwick and was condemned at the shed on 19th February 1966.

**Thursday 12th May 1966. Nottingham (Victoria) station. Stanier Class 5 No.44825 of Colwick shed, makes a dramatic exit from the station with a southbound express. By now most of the motive power using the station comprised Colwick based ex LMS classes such as the Class 5's and the 8F's. BR Standard classes came and went and of course diesel locomotives were in evidence whilst d.m.u.s. had taken over local services. The end for Victoria was not far away.**

*(opposite)* **By request, the driver and fireman of Annesley 9F No.92132 put on this excellent show at the south end of Victoria on Saturday 5th September 1964. Departing from platform 4 the 2-10-0 is at the head of a Skegness Leicester train. After the closure of the ex GNR Leicester (Belgrave Road) station, the Leicester-Skegness trains ran from Leicester (Central) station down the GC main line and reversed in Nottingham (Victoria) to gain the Nottingham - Grantham line to Sleaford and the East Coast. Note the Sheffield based Brush diesel on the middle road which had just brought the train from Skegness.**

*(above and opposite)* **These two pictures tell the story of another 'special', the Locomotive Club of Great Britain's** *THE PENNINE LIMITED RAIL TOUR* **(1X22) on Saturday 19th September 1964. This train arrived from the north behind Stockport Edgeley 'Crab' No.42772 and departed for London behind Crewe North 'Scot' No.46155 THE LANCER (still with nameplates). All this activity was taking place in the evening twilight and when the special left it was practically dark. The 'Scot was days away from a move to Carlisle Kingmoor and just weeks away from oblivion. The 'Crab' would fare slightly better being condemned in the following May.**

(*opposite*) **Just to the south of Victoria station, the running lines became two again to get through the 393 yard long Victoria tunnel in order to reach Weekday Cross junction. Just before the tracks reached the tunnel mouth they had to dive under the bridge which carried Lower Parliament Street over the line. Colwick based Stanier 8F No.48258 has just emerged from the latter bridge and is at the head of a van train making its way south along the GC main on the 14th April 1966. Note the 16C painted where the shed plate should be plus the COLK repeated on the bufferbeam. Colwick shed certainly went to town identifying its own locomotives, LMR origins or not. This 8F arrived at Colwick from Westhouses shed in January 1966 and left Colwick for Edge Hill shed in September of the same year.**

(*right*) **On the 2nd March 1963 I ventured out at midday onto one of the last local trains from Victoria to Sheffield which was hauled by Sheffield Darnall B1 No.61094. Hanging out of the vestibule window of the Gresley carriage I managed to capture this scene before the B1 plunged into an already smoky Mansfield Road tunnel. The sunshine is brilliant but the cold is still sharp with the harsh winter far from over.**

Britannia No.70028, formerly ROYAL STAR, of Crewe South shed heads one of the morning (8.15 a.m.) Nottingham - Marylebone semi-fasts on a sunny Monday 28th June 1965. Why this Pacific was employed on this day is not certain, however, it does emphasise the point that anything could and usually did turn up on these London trains during the latter years of the GC main line.

*(opposite)* The 5.15 p.m. Nottingham (Victoria) to Marylebone semi-fast express was in the hands of Banbury based 'Britannia' No.70052 on Saturday 20th November 1965 and getting near to departure time from platform 10 the engine is ready for the task ahead. Other than the escaping steam, which adds to the eerie scene, there is very little, if any, human activity with neither passengers or staff about the place. Victoria was never a very busy station compared with some other provincial main line stations but this scene resembles more of an 'early hours of the morning' period.

Viewed by two suitably impressed local gentlemen, Annesley 9F No.92067 enters the south end of Victoria's platform 4 (Down fast) with an empty train of steel flats from South Wales to Scunthorpe on 4th July 1964. Through the gloom created by Lower Parliament Street bridge can be seen Nottingham Victoria South signal box which at this time had 95 levers of which about fifteen were spare.

*(opposite)* **On the 10th February 1963 the Home Counties Railway Club ran a special from London to Crewe, returning via Stoke-on-Trent, Eggington Jct., Derby Friargate and Nottingham Victoria to London, using Nine Elms based 'West Country' No.34094 MORTHOE. Here on Victoria's platform 10 the Bullied Pacific takes on water during the return working. The neon advertising of Shipstones Ales glares over the city and adds its statement on this cold winter night.**

Besides the passenger services based on Nottingham Vic., many of the freight trains passing through were headed by Colwick Class 5's. Here 45454 sporting a 2D Banbury shed plate but with a painted COL.K. on both smokebox and bufferbeam pauses with one of the Stanton iron-ore empties. This engine arrived at Colwick in February 1966 and left for Trafford Park in June 1966. What happened to the 2D shed plate?. Note the d.m.u. in platform 7 on a service to Marylebone. In the Up loop 44839 awaits its next job.

(*opposite*) Annesley 9F No.92093 saunters through platform 1 at Victoria with coal empties from Woodford in November 1963. With another twenty months of running these accelerated coal trains between Annesley and Woodford, this 9F was assured employment until the summer of 1965, after which the engine moved on to Kirkby-in-Ashfield shed for a short time before moving on again to Carlisle. Above the York Street bridge can be seen the station clock tower in Trinity Square.

1N63 - the reporting code for the Saturdays Only Poole-Bradford train. The wearing of the reporting number on the front of a locomotive was so important with the Western Region authorities (and bloody useful for trainspotters) and engines from that Region nearly always turned up at Nottingham (Victoria) with some kind of identification on the smokebox, be it chalked on, or it comprised a board with black letters on pasted white paper. However, 1N63 brought something different to Nottingham in the shape of ex-GWR 'Halls' which at the time were very welcome and made a change to the usual diet of the few exLNER and the by now overwhelming diet of exLMS engines which frequented the place. Here we have three separate Western Region engines on three different dates and at different locations within the station. *(left, top)* On Saturday 22nd August 1964, 'Hall' 6906 CHICHELEY HALL has just uncoupled from the Poole-Bradford and having cleared the platform is now reversing along the middle road between platforms 4 and 7, making its way to the turntable and servicing yard on the Up side of the station at the south end. *(left, bottom)* One week later, 6925 HACKNESS HALL has just uncoupled from N63 in platform 1, and runs towards Mansfield Road tunnel to enable it to reverse onto the middle road and run down to the south end. Our old friend, 'Jubilee' 45562 ALBERTA waits on the Down Goods road for the 'Hall' to clear the platform before it sets back, ready to take the train northwards onto Bradford. *(opposite)* The third successive Saturday, 5th September, brings a 'Modified Hall' this time in the shape of 7912 LITTLE LINFORD HALL. Its nice to see the interest which this working brought and its also nice to see nameplates still in situ on the locomotives concerned at so late a date.

Bay platform 3 was a convenient place to stable engines waiting for their trains to arrive. Stanier Class 5's Nos.44825 and 45234 present an impressive sight on Friday 27th May 1966 with lots of available steam. In platform 8 another d.m.u. terminates after working a service from Grantham.

*(opposite)* This portrait of Colwick based 44936 coupling to coaching stock on the 27th May 1966, shows so much of the beauty and grandeur of Nottingham's Victoria station. The station had been opened officially just three days and sixty-six years previously by a company which had such high hopes of making this, and its main line, the showpiece and pacesetter for the twentieth century. Alas, the grandeur and potential of Nottingham Victoria station was never realised and its closure and demolition in 1967 was both swift and brutal. Like so much of what we took for granted, and indeed even held dear, this monumental spaciousness and masterpiece of Victorian determination and enterprise is no more.

**Class 5 No.44839** stands in the Up loop at midday on 12th May 1966 during a lull in the proceedings at the station. From this vantage point we can see the bulk of the station's own hotel - the Victoria what else. Two water columns, with attendant braziers await their last winter of possible use. The station was fast approaching the period of 'the last this, that, and the other.'

When Stanier Class 5 No.45292 rolled into Victoria during the early evening of that historic Saturday 3rd September 1966, (it had brought in the 4.38 p.m. from Marylebone to Nottingham) it was suitably embellished with smokebox graffiti announcing what was what, although once again the crowds are noticeable in their absence. At the time this engine was Tyseley based and it still had more than a years work left in it before it was condemned in November 1967. The chalked reference to Annesley shed on the bufferbeam was something of a mysteryat the time because Annesley shed was closed by this date, and 45292 never had been an Annesley engine, but further research has brought to light the fact that 45292 had spent so much time at Annesley, being serviced, etc., that the few remaining staff had adopted the engine as their own, which begs the question - when did Annesley actually close.

*(opposite)* **On Saturday 3rd September 1966, the 'last ones' came with a flourish to Victoria but went mainly unheralded. The last Nottingham to Marylebone express was assembled and brought into platform 10 by Black 5 No.44984 ready for a 5.15 p.m. departure, which went largely unnoticed by most people. Although the engine wears a wreath of sorts, the general public went about their business blissfully unaware, like they usually do anywhere, that a chapter in Nottingham's history was closing. With the last services would come the rapid run down of the station and then the almost obscene speed with which the developers demolished the station to make way for the building of the Victoria shopping centre. The Class 5, although an LMS engine when it was built in October 1946, had always been associated with the London - Nottingham railway corridor. Its first shed was Kentish Town from where it would work on the St Pancras-Nottingham (Midland) services. In June 1956 it moved to Bedford and then in January 1960 onto exGC lines at Neasden. In March 1962 Leicester GC shed had it until May of the following year when it returned to Bedford for a few weeks before moving down to Cricklewood. In February 1964 it left the former LMS lines for good and went back to Leicester GC for five months and then in July moved north to Annesley. In January 1966 it made its last move, this time to Colwick. In November 1966 it was condemned at Colwick shed and went for scrap to Cashmores yard at Great Bridge in April 1967.**

**Our last look at Nottingham Victoria, albeit a melancholy one. It is April 1968 and except for the two tracks left in situ on the east side of the site, to service the Stanton Ironworks iron ore traffic and some coal trains, the station has been completely swept away as if it never existed. The BR Sulzer Type 2 diesel, complete with a brake tender, has charge of a coal train en route to Colwick for onward transit to the Eastern Counties.**

One of Colwick's grubby fleet of B1's eases an Engineer's train out of the Mansfield Road tunnel and into the daylight before it then plunges into the 665 yard long Sherwood Rise tunnel. The Down platform of the erstwhile station here had long ago lost its platform edge coping and the footbridge which spanned the tracks up to closure of the station in 1928. Some of the buildings are remarkably intact; the street level booking hall and the former station masters house, both visible above the tender, have long since been let out to private enterprise. During the 1990s the old buildings were demolished and this cutting was filled in.

*(opposite)* **Considering this Immingham based B1 No.61406 had not been near a locomotive works for nearly two years, it was looking remarkably well in this April 1965 view at Carrington station. The engine has charge of a coal train, bound no doubt for Colwick yard, but how it got onto this Tuesday working is not known. Emerging from Sherwood Rise tunnel, with the 1896 proclamation centred on the parapet, the train is drifting down grades which varied from 1 in 130 to 1 in 264 on its way to Weekday Cross junction. The Down line is signalled and anything could emerge from the 1189 yard long Mansfield Road tunnel.**

*(opposite)* **On Tuesday 11th May 1965 one of the Annesley-Woodford 'runners' is caught between tunnels at Carrington with Annesley 9F No.92013 in charge. This was the last summer for these accelerated goods trains and by July they would become pure history. This 9F was one of the first of its kind to be allocated to Annesley and eventually the shed had one of the largest fleets in the country just for working the Woodford trains. No.92013 was reallocated to Banbury in June and the start of the end for these trains, and Annesley shed, had set in. All freight working between Quainton Road and Leicester ceased as from Monday 14th June 1965.**

**Captured at the same spot but on 6th April, WD 90036 runs through Carrington with another Engineers train. Looking typically like a WD once the paint shop shine had worn off, this engine had spent most of its life at Colwick shed and was to end it there, being condemned on 19th December 1965.**

Another Annesley 9F, this time 92014, emerges from the Mansfield Road bore at Carrington with empty coal wagons from Woodford. Shortly after this trip the 2-10-0 moved from Annesley to Birkenhead shed where it worked for another two and a half years before being condemned. This photograph has been chosen because it shows the eighteen lever signal box at Carrington, and the colour light signals on the Up side platform. In December 1966 the box was destroyed by fire but no replacement was built nor was necessary. Whilst trains were still stopping at New Basford station, any packages or notices for Carrington signal box were first sent to New Basford where the station staff tied them to a suitable piece of wood and then given to the guard of the next Up train. New Basford box would then tell Carrington box to expect an impending delivery. On passing through the Up platform the guard would then throw the object out of his window to land as near to the signal box as possible for the Bobby to retreive it!

The midday and early afternoon sun was doing its job on 6th April 1965, highlighting each train as they spent a few precious seconds between the murky depths of the tunnels at Carrington. O4/8 No.63873 had been at Colwick shed since June 1954 but before that it had spent time on GC main line sheds at Woodford and Annesley so was no stranger to these particular bores. Here it has charge of a Colwick bound coal train probably originating from one of the Leen valley collieries. Note the signals, Down Starter and New Basford Distant are again off for a Down working.

A last look at one of the 'runners' passing through Carrington's long deserted platforms. No.92090 has a full brake in tow immediately behind the tender (this was included to increase the locomotive's braking power as certain trains had been speeded up) as it hurtles southward during the last summer of these trains. This view gives the reader an idea of the amount of rock removed by the builders of the last main line at this one small station, as the new railway approached Nottingham centre.

K3's were, to coin a phrase "common as muck" around Nottingham before September 1962. Colwick had a sizeable allocation from the earliest days so these engines were well known. On the 16th September 1962 all the K3's still operational at Colwick were condemned - another class had worked its last around Nottingham. No.61914 was at New Basford with an Up fitted goods train on the 1st August 1962 and it too was working out its final days but this engine was condemned before the others on Thursday 23rd August 1962. This picture was one of my very first and many thousands more were to be exposed over the remaining years of steam on Britain's railways.

The last steam hauled Bournemouth-York express ran on Saturday 8th September 1962 with V2 No.60921 having charge of the train to its destination. York V2's were regular performers on this train and they were going to be missed, however, there were plenty of other York V2's working into and through the Nottingham area during the remaining years of their existence. No.60921 has just exited Sherwood Rise tunnel and is climbing the 1 in 130 to New Basford with plenty to spare.

**Thompson's L1 2-6-4T was another popular class of engine around Nottingham in the 1950's and right up to the end of 1962 when suddenly on 29th December the sixteen survivors were all condemned at Colwick shed marking the extinction of the class. No.67798, here at New Basford on 1st December is heading towards Nottingham (Victoria) bunker first with a train from Derby (Friargate).**

**The last train from Pinxton to Nottingham (Victoria) ran on the evening of Saturday 5th January 1963 and Colwick B1 No.61299 was suitably decked out for the occasion. Why bunting is used to celebrate both joy and, in this case, sadness, is one of the mysteries of mankind. The winter of 1962-63 was one of the coldest on record and this photograph captures perfectly the ambience of the period. The driver had been asked previously if he would stop the engine at the 'line' in the snow so that I would get the correct exposure - as you can see it worked.**

Night photography was not something to be taken lightly, especially in mid February 1963 but this scene at new Basford carriage sidings on the 11th of that month certainly was worth recording if only for its atmosphere. The Colwick breakdown train has arrived behind ex-LMS 2-6-0 No.43145 to attend to Class 5 No.45234 which had derailed on the crossover just visible in the photograph. Between the engine and the crane was the crew riding van which consisted of an old eight-wheel coach of pre-Group origins. The crane is the Cowans Sheldon 36 tonner which had been allocated to Colwick since 1936 when it arrived new from its makers. I presented a copy of this photograph to the breakdown crew a few days later and it was duly framed by the shed joiner and was hung up in the van. When Colwick shed closed this crane did a stint at Toton and then Newton Heath depots before being purchased for preservation.

As mentioned earlier, V2's were fairly plentiful around Nottingham in 1962 and 1963 as witnessed by York based 60886 on a Nottingham - Chesterfield - Sheffield local, stopping at New Basford on Saturday 16th February 1963. Beyond the engine, at a slightly lower level is the goods yard with two rows of passenger coaching stock using up available space. Although the Station Master at Basford North was in charge of New Basford also, he had a lady 'deputy' (senior Porter) named Lily who looked after the proceedings at New Basford during the morning and afternoon. She was always helpful and kindly to me, always looking after my safety.

Another York V2, No.60895 soaks up the late afternoon sun at New Basford carriage sidings on 16th March 1963. The engine has the stock of the 5.15 p.m. Nottingham-Marylebone. If a 'Green Arrow' happened to be standing spare on Annesley shed it was more often than not purloined for a run to Marylebone and back - after all, a V2 in any condition was always a better bet than one of the depots' own run down 'Royal Scots'.

At about 6.47 p.m. on most weekday evenings, another York V2 turn brought the Banbury-York fitted freight through New Basford station and Monday 10th June 1963 was no exception as 60805 makes a bit of smoke on its climbs towards Bagthorpe Junction.

*(opposite)* **Perry Road overbridge at New Basford was a superb vantage point from which to watch and photograph trains. At about midday on a Saturday in April 1963, 'Royal Scot' 46111 ROYAL FUSILIER meets with Colwick WD 90438 on the embankment at New Basford. The WD is taking coal empties back to the mines whilst the 'Scot' is making its way to Nottingham (Victoria) to take an express to Marylebone. Note that the carriage sidings have a couple of engines in the yard, a Black 5 and a B1. 46111 was one of fifteen 'Royal Scots' which Annesley shed acquired between 1962 and 1964 to work Great Central line expresses. Most of them finished their working days at Annesley including 46111 which arrived in January 1963 and was condemned during the following September. To say that the LMR had had the best from these engines would be an understatement and according to Annesley footplatemen the 'Scots' were rough riders. They "were bloody awful" according to one old boy who used to have two pieces of clothes line in his overalls pocket so that he could tie himself to the cab handrail in a bid to survive each trip. One ruse nearly always used by crews on the 5.15 p.m. Marylebone semi-fast was to arrive at New Basford to pick up the stock for a 4.15 p.m. departure down to Victoria. Before leaving the carriage sidings the fireman would load coal into the firebox as high as the brick arch so that by the time of departure from Victoria at 5.15 the fire would be perfect and would last as far as Leicester all being well. Firing at speed on one of the Annesley Scots was certainly not recommended.**

To see so many V2's together in these pages where there were previously none gives a fair idea of the traffic patterns and photographic opportunities available in the early 1960's. Here, on Saturday 15th June 1963, yet another York V2, 60967 has the empty stock of the 5.15 Marylebone semi-fast at New Basford carriage sidings. The 'Crab', 42896, is from Nottingham Midland shed and had arrived with empty stock and will soon depart back to 16A no doubt via the exchange sidings between the GN lines at London Road High Level and the LMS lines at Low Level.

*(opposite)* **On a superbly warm evening York V2 No.60939 makes light work with this northbound goods train up the bank out of New Basford on the 9th August 1963. At this time the 2-6-2s were fairly common on the GC main line, at least in Nottinghamshire, and although most of them were York engines, that shed had a very large allocation so it was reasonable to expect a different engine with each sighting.**

Night photography can be rewarding if patience holds out. Here at New Basford carriage sidings, in March 1964, Class 5 No.45349 simmers in the cold darkness, surrounded by an eerie but nevertheless welcoming halo of steam. The cab warmly lit up by the glow given off when the firebox door is opened. Note the stars adding their magical glow to the scene.

Having recently arrived at Annesley shed from Crewe North, 'Royal Scot' 46165 THE RANGER was the last of its kind to inhabit the Great Central route. Before 46165 got to Annesley shed most of the previous batch of 'Scots' working from Annesley had been condemned and during its nine month sojourn all the others except for 46122 were withdrawn. However, 46122 was reallocated to Carlisle Upperby in October 1964 but 46122 was condemned in the same month and probably never left Annesley anyway - add on the fact that 46122 went for scrap to Drapers of Hull in February 1965 and it seems certain that the 'Scot' never left for Upperby shed after all. Now THE RANGER was the last Royal Scot allocated to Annesley and was due to return to Crewe North shed by official reallocation in November 1964 but it too was condemned in that same month, it went for scrap to T.W.Ward at Beighton in March 1965, virtually a local yard to Annesley. So, in conclusion, all fifteen Royal Scot 4-6-0's shedded at Annesley seem to have also ended their days there too. Back to this picture, 46165, now minus nameplate, it on 1T08 which was either a schoolboy international football match or hockey international at Wembley.

Farnley Junction 'Jubilee' No.45562 ALBERTA was a regular performer on the Poole-Bradford trains from Nottingham and on 25th July 1964 the engine, looking impressively clean, heads the train through New Basford shortly after exiting Sherwood Rise tunnel. On the right is the two storey goods warehouse built to service the needs of the district when the line opened - by now the goods facility here was doing very little if anything and would soon close.

*(opposite)* Colwick B1 No.61141 is on the last leg of a Saturdays only Skegness - Derby train (reporting number 1M32) in May 1964. It is early evening as the train climbs the bank from New Basford up to Bagthorpe Junction where it will diverge left and take the line westward through Basford & Bulwell. By this time diesel multiple units had taken over most of the local services and New Basford carriage shed was planned as a fuelling base for the units. The diesel fuel tanks can be seen in the yard immediately above the second and third coaches of the Derby train. The scheme for fuelling local d.m.u.s. came to nothing and it is doubtful that those tanks were ever filled with oil.

**6858 WOOLSTON GRANGE passing New Basford at the start of its 'epic' journey north to Huddersfield in August 1964 (*see* description elsewhere). "No more platforms now for at least a couple of miles" might be one of the thoughts going through the drivers' mind but there again he was an Annesley man and they would drive anything as long as it had steam.**

Being a resident of Basford nowadays must seem fairly quiet perhaps when compared with the latter days of the exGC main line. On 1st August 1964, 'Jubilee' No.45562 ALBERTA, which is no stranger to these pages, was doing its best to make the local populace aware of its being as it climbs the 1 in 130 bank northwards out of New Basford.

56

On Sunday 6th September 1964 British Railways ran the last of their trains from New Basford to Skegness, Mablethorpe and everywhere else for that matter. The motive power for the occasion was to be this diesel-electric D1564 from Immingham shed. Note the cast shed plate on the bottom edge of the yellow warning panel. The early morning sun casts shadows on the platform as the train ambles in for its first stop.

**One can almost shiver looking at this view of Colwick O4/8 No.63674 passing New Basford, with an Up coal train, in March 1965. Although there has been only a light snow fall, the cold has prevented any thaw and the temperature was hovering around freezing.**

**Another meeting on the bank at New Basford, this time between two WD's and both heading mineral trains on Wednesday 12th May 1965. On the Up line an unidentified and grubby Colwick engine heads a heavy coal train tender first towards the station, as an equally grubby 90438 slogs up the bank with a heavy iron ore train bound for Stanton's works near Ilkeston. A copy of this photograph, lent to a friend a while ago to illustrate an article about Colwick engine shed caused the driver Ernest Yardley, then all of 83 years old, to recognise himself and promptly ask if he could get a copy.**

**On Monday morning 10th May 1965, preserved A3 N.4472 FLYING SCOTSMAN was travelling 'light' en route to Doncaster through New Basford station. With no load except its own weight, the engine has left hardly any exhaust behind in Sherwood Rise tunnel and this enables us to see through the gloom to Carrington.**

The carriage shed at New Basford consisted of six roads under three roof bays, each bay having the profile of a Dutch barn. The shed had been built in time for the opening of Victoria station and with the shed came an oil gas works, the chimney of which dominated the immediate area. Stanier Class 5 No.45379 of Willesden shed had the empty stock of the 5.15 p.m. to Marylebone on 12th May 1965 and is about to join the Up line for the run down to Victoria station.

**9F No.92067, with a painted smokebox number, drifts through New Basford on the 25th May 1965 with a Woodford bound coal train. These trains will soon finish as preparations to end GC line services are gradually coming to fruition. In the next couple of weeks 92067 will move away from Annesley, its home for the last eight years, and be reallocated to Banbury from where it will work out its final days.**

After turning on the triangle at Bagthorpe Junction, ex GWR 6861 CRYNANT GRANGE, carrying neither name or cab side number plates, drifts down the bank past the carriage sheds at New Basford on its way back to Victoria on 26th June 1965. The engine is in a deplorable state externally which was usual for the period.

*(opposite)* The Stanlow - Colwick oil train usually brought a Birkenhead 9F to Nottingham and after a service on Colwick shed the same engine would work the empty train back to Cheshire. On 9th June 1965 ex-Crosti 9F No.92020 attempts to blacken the evening sky as it climbs the bank at New Basford with the Colwick - Stanlow empties.

Banbury shed was responsible, in the latter years of the GC main line, for supplying the locomotive which hauled the 5.15 p.m. Nottingham (Victoria) to Marylebone semi-fast. Ideally suited for the job in question were the eight Britannia Pacifics which the shed acquired in September 1965. These 'Brits', Nos.70045 to 70047 and 70050 to 70054, were all fitted with the BR1D tender, a tender type only found with 70045 to 70054, at first. The BR1D tender had a capacity of nine tons of coal, besides 4,725 gallons of water, but it is the former figure which interests us here. The nine tons coal capacity allowed the Banbury 'Brits' to complete a circuit from Banbury to Annesley to Marylebone and back to Banbury without refuelling. To make life even cushier for the fireman, each tender was equipped with a steam powered coal pusher. Alas, Banbury shed lost its 'Brits' in January 1966. However, during that period of plenty, on 9th October 1965, at approximately 4.15 p.m., by now unnamed 70052, previously FIRTH OF TAY, was at New Basford carriage sidings heading the stock of the 5.15 p.m. Marylebone express, exiting the sidings for Victoria station with chime whistle sounding. These impressive machines, although 70052 looks less than cared for here, had once been associated with a GC line shed when, from June to October 1962, Nos.70014, 70015, 70048 and 70049 were allocated to Annesley for workings such as this. Of course Annesley lost its 'Brits' to Willesden in favour of the run-down 'Scots'.

(*opposite*) With a fair bit of weight pushing down the 1 in 130 towards Sherwood Rise tunnel, Colwick WD No.90669 trundles past the photographer with the Stanlow - Colwick oil train on 2nd October 1965. Note the BR1D tender of a Britannia on the goods yard headshunt.

On occasion Annesley shed was so short of motive power that any engine no matter how unsuitable would be turned out on any duty (a one-cylinder only working Black 5 No.44932 was once turned out on a local pick-up job). This is how unnamed Banbury 'Britannia' 70047 was found on 9th October 1965 shunting New Basford goods yard. Incidentally if there was something unusual - like a 'Brit' shunting - this would be accompanied by a lot of chime whistling instigated by the local shunter who hoped that I had been alerted and would soon show up with camera at the ready. This view gives us a chance to see some more of the goods shed with its twin awnings and well illuminated upper floor. These facilities closed shortly after the passenger station closed but they had been little used since the late 1950s.

It wasn't just Colwick's engines suffering from lack of cleaning in the 1960's. This Ivatt 'mogul' No.43115, a stranger from Stoke, is hardly looking its best on the 16th October 1965 as it passes through the derelict and closed New Basford station with a mineral train, probably headed for Colwick yard. Minus its numberplate, shedplate and heavily stained the 2-6-0 looks about ready for the scrapyard but it was to be nearly two years before this engine was condemned in June 1967.

In this view from Perry Road bridge on 27th May 1966, Stanier 8F 48258, another 1966 Colwick import seems to be making light work of this loaded Stanton bound iron-ore train up the 1 in 130 towards Bagthorpe Junction. The 8F went to Colwick in January and then left there for Edge Hill shed in September.

As 1966 dawned the former GC main line around Nottingham began to appear more like an LMS line. Stanier 8F No.48645 of Colwick shed - note the double ID - drifts down the 1 in 130 from Bagthorpe Junction, towards New Basford, with what seems to be a pick-up for brake vans on the 19th March 1966. Probably this lot were en route to Colwick yard to join the throng already there for storage. Perry Road bridge, the vantage point for so many of my photographs, appears in the immediate background. Note the blast plates suspended at least a yard below the underside of the bridge.

Towards the end of steam working in the Nottingham area, the Stanton iron ore trains originating off the Denton branch were hauled mainly by Colwick B1's and many of the Thompson 4-6-0s at Colwick had a longer lease of life because of those workings. In May 1965 No.61302 takes a train of empties through Bagthorpe cutting heading back to the quarry.

When 'Royal Scot' No.46112 arrived at Annesley in September 1962, it had not travelled far having been resident in the city since December 1959 at the former Midland shed. However, in this Saturday 29th September 1962 photograph, taken at Perry Road bridge, the engine is without its SHERWOOD FORESTER nameplates. By 1962 the 'Scots' had been around for a long time and during their lives they had put in a lot of mileage so were fairly run down. Add to that, the fact that major repairs on this class had virtually ceased and you have the perfect recipe for a 'boneshaker'. 46112 was condemned at Annesley in May 1964 and cut up at Cashmores, Great Bridge at the end of that same summer. The little boy standing at the fence could have been me eight years previously.

**23rd May 1964, Perry Road bridge, north side. With plenty to spare, O4 No.63913 and a lime train, passing through the rock cutting which separated New Basford from Bagthorpe Junction. Note the excellent condition of the permanent way which was, after all, still a main line.**

Still at Perry Road in 1964, and 'Crab' 42827 is waiting at the signals - light engine and brakevan. The 'Crab' was at the time a Birkenhead engine and what it was doing in Nottingham on Saturday 19th September is anybody's guess but it could have been en route to Colwick to collect empty oil tanks after repair.

30th April 1966 was a glorious Spring day and just about noon a Stanier 8F, 48192 is making its way light back to Colwick shed after its work. Of course diesel as well as steam locomotives used this line and although we haven't witnessed both of them, two transitions have taken place on the GC route; one, the diesels have arrived and gradually taken over many of the services but the other transition, from exLNER to exLMS, was more of an overnight thing and by early 1966 the LNER types were no more and the LMS types reigned supreme - at least for a while and then they too would disappear along with the railway.

(opposite) **Bagthorpe cutting, Saturday 27th April 1963.** What a combination - Robinson O4/8 plus an ex LMS 'Royal Scot' on a freight train on the former GC main line. The O4/8 is 63675, a Colwick engine. The Scot, 46163 CIVIL SERVICE RIFLEMAN, was recently allocated to Annesley shed from Willesden in exchange for Britannia's - Annesley got the raw deal. No.46163 was sent to Annesley in January but it is still wearing a 1A shed plate. By August of the following year this 'Scot' will be history but the O4/8 will be good for another eighteen months before it was withdrawn, prematurely, by the London Midland authorities when they took over at Colwick shed. Line occupancy round about lunchtime was very tight, most trains being "on the block" all the way to Victoria station. 46163 was making its way 'light' for a midday working to London from Victoria, so the enterprising Bobby at Bagthorpe Junction coupled it onto the front of 63675 on a returning empty iron ore train, and sent them both through together.

In 1963 one working guaranteed to produce an Immingham 'Britannia' was the evening New Clee to Banbury fish train, passing Bagthorpe Junction at about 7.30 p.m. On Thursday 8th August, however, disaster struck. A spirited run down the bank from Bulwell to Bagthorpe Junction (it was probably a little behind time) resulted in the guard deciding that a touch of handbrake was in order. However, the resultant drag on the rear section of the train resulted in a snapped coupling and the train parting about one third from the rear, leaving that rear portion stranded near to Bagthorpe whilst the rest of the train, headed by No.70037 HEREWARD THE WAKE, came to a stand by the Up starting signal at Perry Road bridge. With commendable speed 70037 departed for New Basford signal box, set back and deposited the defective fish van in the carriage sidings, pulled forward to the box, where they reset the carriage siding point to enable the 'Brit' and the rest of its train to set back 'wrong road' all the way to Bagthorpe box to pick up the rest of the train, couple up and be on its way again.

It was always nice to see a 'foreign' B1 knocking about, even better if it was one of the named engines. Ardsley B1 No.61215 WILLIAM HENTON CARVER came down from the north with this train of steel slabs and what looks like graded scrap, no doubt bound for South Wales on the 11th April 1964. Except for the 16-ton coal wagon on the front of the train the rest of the wagons consist of bogie flat wagons.

**Stanier Class 5 No.44920 of Colwick shed negotiates Bagthorpe cutting in May 1966 with a short parcels train. This view shows off well the sandstone rock formation which the 'navvies' of the 1890's had to cut through in order to keep the gradients of the new railway reasonable.**

Getting near to the top of the 1 in 130 climb from New Basford, Stanier 8F No.48323 arrives at Bagthorpe Junction on 27th May 1966 with a train of empty cattle wagons. Livestock movements by trains were at one time the established method of transporting animals and tens of thousands per week would be railbourne up to the mid 1950's. When road transportation of livestock started to take over, its governing rules were not as stringent as those by which the railways had to abide and so within a decade 'livestock by rail' was unheard of and BR lost another customer.

B1's 61173 and 61131 rattle over Bagthorpe Junction with the returning LCGB Last Day Great Central Rail Tour excursion to Marylebone via Nottingham (Victoria) on the 3rd September 1966. This view gives the reader an idea of the undulating nature of the topography in this district of Nottingham. Perry Road bridge links the high ground where the railway sliced through the rock strata some seventy-odd years previously.

In less than a mile from the northern portal of Sherwood Rise tunnel the GC main line passes through a deep cutting, sweeps past a goods yard and associated shed, runs over an embankment, through an island platform station, over a busy thoroughfare, past a carriage shed and its yard, up another embankment, into another cutting, this one spanned by a road bridge, out onto an embankment before meeting a junction and eventually levelling out after a continuos climb. On the way two signal boxes were passed. Another few hundred yards further on and more carriage sidings would be seen, a locomotive turntable, another main line passing from west to east; junctions going off in all directions with burrowing lines and bridges (*see also* Part Two). That description of but a small portion of the Great Central Main Line could easily be used by a railway modeller to describe a layout many of us would perhaps like to build and operate. The mile in question could easily be scaled down to 4mm/1ft and then built to fit around an average room but, would fellow modellers say that its a bit too fussy to be prototypical - too much in said mile? Its funny how the full size blokes always seen to have done it first.

**The symmetry of Bagthorpe Junction, is apparent in this view from the cab of Stanier 5 No.45234 as it heads northwards up the GC main in May 1965.** *(Chris Ward)*

As mentioned earlier, the East Midlands branch of the RCTS organised an annual rail tour to one of BR's locomotive works. In October 1963 the destination was Horwich works, via Crewe works, and the appropriate motive power for the occasion was Hughes/Fowler 'Crab' No.42896 of Nottingham Midland shed. As the participants make their way to their seats, John Henton has a word with Inspector Reg Haynes who will be in charge throughout the trip. Notice the excellent manner in which the engine has been turned out. In the background can be seen the girders of the GC bridge.

Night photography does not figure greatly in this album but the inclusion of this exposure seemed necessary to give some balance to the locomotive types illustrated within these pages. Ex-LMS 4F No.44113, of Westhouses shed, is one of the older LMS engines appearing in this book and Crewe built, in 1925, it was withdrawn in 1966 and was amongst the last of its kind. Here, on the 17th October 1965, 44113 is seen in Nottingham (Midland) station [at 6.55 p.m. according to the station clock] with the empty stock, just four carriages, of a Nottingham and Derby local area railtour.

For a few gloriuos weeks in the summer of 1966, a 55C Farnley Junction 'Jubilee' was rostered to work as far as Nottingham (Midland) on the Saturdays Only Bradford-Poole and return (this delight lasted only from 25th June to 3rd September). The 'Jubilee' came off and then went to Colwick shed for servicing and to await the return working. So, for a very brief period a 'Jubilee' had returned to Nottingham (Midland) where years ago they were an everyday sight. Consequently, it became a crusade to photograph the 'visitor' in as many different locations as possible. Allied to the run down and the last trains out of Victoria station, life became hectic for those few weeks. 'Jubilee' 45562 ALBERTA accelerates out of Midland station on the 20th August 1966. The array of semaphore signals is a delight to see as are the sidings, goods vehicles and the general railway infrastructure still evident in the mid 1960s. Over the last thirty-odd years much has changed from this view point. Buildings have been swept aside, land sold, locomotives and stock scrapped, track layouts rationalised and altered drastically. But, Midland station frontage on Carrington Street is still the same.

*(opposite)* On the way out of Midland station, going west, one of the first things noticed was the motive power depot which was, throughout most of its LMS and BR existence, coded 16A. By 1963 it had become subordinate to Toton depot and became 16D, before closing in November 1967. On 27th March 1965, when the diesels were taking over everything, including shed room, this ex Great Western 'Castle' No.7029 CLUN CASTLE called in after rail tour duty. Over the ash pit the 4-6-0 gets an oiling from its driver before proceeding onto one of the shed stabling roads.

At Lenton Junction the Midland line separates with the main line which continues west towards Trent and Derby whilst the other line strikes north and starts to follow the course of the River Leen towards its source. 'Jubilee' 45562 ALBERTA is once again featured, this time heading for the Erewash Valley line, 20th August 1966.

Stanier 8F's were plentiful on the former Midland Railway lines around Nottingham long before they took over at Colwick shed and then saturated the ex LNER lines around the city. Here, on 9th May 1965 at Bobbers Mill (so called after Bobbers corn mill once situated nearby between here and the river Leen), approximately midway between Radford Junction and Basford Vernon, 48156 has a train of empty coal wagons en route to one of the local collieiries served by the exMR Leen Valley line. At this point the River Leen runs to the east of the railway, on the left of the picture the 40-gallon drums seen stored in the right background are to do with one of the local dyeing and bleaching factories of which there were many along this section of the valley. Prior to building Bobbers Mill bridge, the Nuthall/Alfreton Road crossed the railway on a level crossing.

Basford Gas Works stood on the east side of the MR line on Radford Road. In this 27th November 1964 view, 8F 48024 is passing with a loaded coal train, the rear of which is still beneath the bridge carrying Western Boulevard. A little further to the south, just behind the photographer, the River Leen crosses beneath the railway.

(*opposite*) Lincoln Street crossing, 3rd October 1964. Stanier 8F 48045 rumbles across the road with a heavy coal train bound for Staythorpe power station. The 8F had been allocated to Nottingham shed since March and would leave 16D for Westhouses shed in April 1965. This engine was one of those loaned to the War Department in 1942 and reinstated by BR in August 1949. Note the early Stanier tender which had originally been coupled behind a 'Jubilee' 4-6-0. This particular view of the level crossing shows us so much which we may have forgotten about. The motor vehicles, bikes and scooters, gas lamps, gated crossings. The fashion, chrome, people walking, the corner shop and the 44 trolleybus en route to Hall Estate, Bulwell.

Stanier designed, Derby built 1938, Kirkby-in-Ashfield based (just). Ex LMS Class 4MTT No.42618 hurtles through Basford Vernon bunker first towards Nottingham (Midland) on the 8th February 1964 with a train from Mansfield. Note the fleet number on the corridor coach - SC26811M - not the usual numbers associated with coaching stock on this route. This panning shot captures 42618 nicely whilst the blurred surroundings give the illusion of great speed. Kirkby allocated since November 1961, the 4MTT had just a couple of weeks more work in the Nottinghamshire area before it reallocated to Leeds Neville Hill shed in March.

*(opposite)* Except for the coaching stock, virtually every piece of railway infrastructure, furniture and of course the locomotive, is of pure Midland Railway origin. Take the train away and a nice picture of Lincoln Street crossing would have been formed by the lattice construction footbridge, signals, signal box and crossing gates and clear sky. The Workington 4F 0-6-0, suitably 'bulled-up' for the occasion is at the head of another RCTS special (1X20) on 16th October 1965, covering the lines from Nuneaton, through Trent and the mid Leen Valley line northward on local colliery branches.

**Empty coal wagons were always in demand by the collieries right up to the age of merry-go-round. Here at Basford Vernon, on 8th February 1964, Nottingham based 8F No.48638 hauls a long rake of empties up to one of the pits in the Leen Valley. Except for five months in early 1959, this engine spent the whole of its life working from East Midlands sheds such as Toton and Westhouses, from which shed it was withdrawn in January 1966. Note the reporting number 37 - some local workings had target numbers allocated.**

Nottingham based Stanier 8F No.48319 makes the footbridge rumble as it passes through Basford Vernon station on 21st September 1963 with a heavy train of loaded 16-ton steel bodied mineral wagons. The gradient is downhill for most of the way on this side of the city so all the 2-8-0 has to do is keep the train in check. Within two months this engine will have left the area for the North-West, Fleetwood to be precise, and will move on from there to four other depots in the area before eventual withdrawal in March 1968 (this engine's life history follows very much that of 48317 featured on the next page). From this vantage point we get a reasonable view along Vernon Road on the trolleybus route towards the city centre. Nowadays this particular section of railway forms part of the route of the Robin Hood line between Nottingham and Worksop.

Although the weather has changed for the better, nothing else gives any clue that this view of Basford Vernon was captured at a later date than the previous photograph, in fact on 30th May 1964. Another 8F, 48317 of Kirkby-in-Ashfield shed, forms the subject of study as it approaches with coal empties for one of the Leen Valley pits. This engine, one of the wartime builds, was at first sent to Canklow shed in January 1944. It eventually got to Kirkby during May 1959 and left there for Trafford Park shed in February 1967, being withdrawn in March of the following year - just twenty-four years old.